Random Mind Blowing Trivia – 200 Random Multiple Choice Trivia Questions

Volume 1

Copyright 2024

1. Which US state has the longest coastline?

A. Florida

B. California

C. Alabama

D. Alaska

2. Which animal was the first animal in space?

A. Fruit flies

B. dogs

C. monkeys

D. cats

3. What is the longest mountain range in the world?

A. Alaska Range

B. Andes

C. Himalayas

D. Tian Shan

4. In which country is divorce illegal?

A. Philippines

B. Iran

C. Somalia

D. Dominican Republic

5. Which country is NOT part of the Mediterranean?

A. Italy

B. Greece

C. Germany

D. Spain

6. What profession did Spartacus have?

A. Politician

B. Slave

C. Gladiator

D. Farmer

7. Where on the human body is the zygomatic bone found?

A. Eyebrow

B. Pelvis

C. Facial cheek

D. Foot

8. What is the mass of 1 liter of water?

A. 100 grams

B. 1 kilogram

C. 1 pint

D. 1 pound

9. Which country invented paper?

A. China

B. Japan

C. USA

D. Spain

10. What is the lowest army rank of a US soldier?

A. Private

B. Corporal

C. Specialist

D. Sergeant

11. Hepatitis is inflammation of which organ?

A. brain

B. kidney

C. liver

D. lung

12. Which is the closest star to earth?

A. Alpha Centauri

B. Proxima Centauri

C. Sirius

D. Sun

13. Who was the longest-serving U.K. Prime Minister?

A. Robert Walpole

B. William Pitt

C. Tony Blair

D. David Cameron

14. In Roman Myth Mars is the god of what?

A. Games

B. love

C. war

D. law

15. Who developed the theory of relativity?

A. Marie Curie

B. Albert Einstein

C. Stephen Hawking

D. Isaac Newton

16. What is the largest continent by population?

A. Europe

B. Asia

C. Africa

D. North America

17. Who was monarch after Queen Elizabeth I?

A. Henry VI

B. George II

C. Victoria

D. James VI

18. Where is the Machu Picchu located?

A. Nepal

B. Brazil

C. Peru

D. Myanmar

19. How many brains does a starfish have?

A. 0

B. 1

C. 2

D. 5

20. What country was formerly referred to as Persia?

A. Egypt

B. Iran

C. Greece

D. Italy

21. In which city does the queen live?

A. London

B. Edinburgh

C. Manchester

D. Bristol

22. Who was the first U.S Secretary of Treasury?

A. Alexander Hamilton

B. John Adams

C. Aaron Burr

D. Thomas Edison

23. Which US state is also called the Aloha State?

A. Hawaii

B. Arizona

C. Colorado

D. Delaware

24. Which gas makes the bubbles in a soda drink?

A. argon

B. carbon dioxide

C. nitrogen

D. oxygen

25. Who was the cartoonist behind the Far Side Gallery?

A. Scott Adams

B. Robert Crumb

C. Gary Larson

D. Walt Disney

26. How many time zones does the United States have?

A. 12

B. 9

C. 5

D. 14

27. How many faces does a dodecahedron have?

A. 10

B. 12

C. 16

D. 20

28. How many republics were part of the Soviet Union?

A. 12

B. 20

C. 15

D. 10

29. Which is the smallest organ in the human body?

A. appendix

B. gall bladder

C. pineal gland

D. spleen

30. Distance is equal to speed multiplied by what?

A. acceleration

B. length

C. time

D. velocity

31. The Mayans worshiped which animal as gods?

A. Horses

B. cats

C. rabbits

D. turkeys

32. Charles Darwin is famous for the theory of what?

A. continental drift

B. evolution

C. relativity

D. the big bang

33. What type of tree grows from an acorn?

A. elm

B. fir

C. maple

D. oak

34. Which of these numbers is larger?

A. billion

B. centillion

C. googol

D. trillion

35. What country did the U.S. buy Alaska from?

A. Canada

B. Mexico

C. England

D. Russia

36. Bicycles were first used in which country?

A. Germany

B. Thailand

C. France

D. Denmark

37. What is the Jewish New Year called?

A. Shabbat

B. Hanukkah

C. Yom Kippur

D. Rosh Hashanah

38. How many years old is the oldest piece of chewing gum?

A. 2,500 years

B. 11,000 years

C. 9,000 years

D. 6,000 years

39. What was banned in Indonesia for stimulating passion?

A. Chocolate

B. Pop music

C. Hula hoops

D. Coca-cola

40. Which country has the highest agricultural production?

A. China

B. Brazil

C. Australia

D. Russia

41. Who invented the rocking chair?

A. Thomas Edison

B. Nikola Tesla

C. Thomas Jefferson

D. Benjamin Franklin

42. What is a haboob?

A. A type of savory pie

B. A type of sandstorm

C. A type of bird

D. A person who forgets things

43. Nepal is located on which continent?

A. Asia

B. Africa

C. Oceania

D. South America

44. In 1979 the USSR invaded which country?

A. China

B. Iran

C. Afghanistan

D. Ukraine

45. What language has the most words?

A. French

B. English

C. Chinese

D. Hindi

46. What did Alexander Graham Bell
invent?

A. doorbell

B. lightbulb

C. telephone

D. television

47. How did Fredrick Douglass escape slavery?

A. Ran away

B. Underground Railroad

C. disguised as a sailor

D. murder

48. Which date was Julius Caesar killed?

A. March 15th

B. March 30th

C. February 15th

D. March 17th

49. Hemoglobin contains which metal?

A. copper

B. iron

C. lead

D. silver

50. Who was the Iron Lady?

A. Theresa May

B. Meryl Streep

C. Margaret Thatcher

D. Carol Thatcher

51. What does the Scoville scale measure?

A. brightness of light

B. hardness of rocks

C. strength of earthquakes

D. spiciness of chili peppers

52. What country has competitive office chair racing?

A. Thailand

B. Japan

C. Chile

D. Canada

53. What's the brightest star in the sky?

A. Vega

B. Sirius

C. Capella

D. Altair

54. Which Philosopher tutored Alexander the Great?

A. Plato

B. Isocrates

C. Ptolemy

D. Aristotle

55. Who did Aaron Burr kill?

A. Abraham Lincoln

B. Alexander Hamilton

C. George Washington

D. Thomas Jefferson

56. In which city did Anne Frank hide from the Nazis?

A. Berlin

B. Paris

C. Warsaw

D. Amsterdam

57. Galileo was the citizen of which country?

A. France

B. Portugal

C. Italy

D. Germany

58. Caesar salad originated from which country?

A. Italy

B. Mexico

C. France

D. Italy

59. Which city was the ASPCA founded in?

A. New York City

B. Pittsburgh

C. Denver

D. Chicago

60. Madras is now called as which Indian city?

A. Chennai

B. Kolkata

C. Jaipur

D. Surat

61. Where did the Battle of Stalingrad take place?

A. Germany

B. Soviet Union

C. Poland

D. France

62. What year did the Spanish civil war occur?

A. 1920

B. 1930

C. 1936

D. 1940

63. Which country has a flag with only two colors?

A. India

B. Italy

C. Germany

D. Nigeria

64. What is often seen as the smallest unit of memory?

A. GigaByte

B. MegaByte

C. TeraByte

D. kilobyte

65. The oldest living person lived in which country?

A. France

B. Japan

C. Italy

D. USA

66. The United Kingdom shares a border with which country?

A. Spain

B. Ireland

C. France

D. Norway

67. Julius Caesar was kidnapped by who in 78 BC?

A. Senate

B. pirates

C. enemy nation

D. family

68. Which Germany Official ordered the Final Solution?

A. Hitler

B. Goering

C. Himmler

D. Heydrich

69. How many countries have names that
end in -stan?

A. 10

B. 5

C. 8

D. 7

70. An Apgar score is given to what?

A. Graduate students

B. Health of newborns

C. Velocity of an object in a vacuum

D. Acidity in drinks

71. The term malar refers to what part of the human body?

A. cheek

B. feet

C. lung

D. toes

72. Who introduced the world's first mass-produced car?

A. Louis Chevrolet

B. Walter Chrysler

C. Henry Ford

D. William Durant

73. Which fruit floats because 25% of its volume is air?

A. Pomegranate

B. Honeydew

C. Strawberry

D. Apple

74. What does an ornithologist study?

A. birds

B. ears

C. mushrooms

D. organs

75. What are the two fruit juices in a cosmopolitan?

A. Cranberry and lemon

B. Orange and cranberry

C. Cranberry and lime

D. Pineapple and coconut

76. Where did Barack Obama teach constitutional law?

A. University of Chicago

B. University of Illinois

C. Northwestern University

D. Loyola University

77. Which University did Karl Marx attend in 1835?

A. London

B. Paris

C. Brussels

D. Bonn

78. What is the world's biggest rodent?

A. beaver

B. capybara

C. porcupine

D. rat

79. If a male donkey is a jack what is the female called?

A. Jackie

B. Regina

C. Jane

D. Jenny

80. The space race was between the U.S. and which country?

A. France

B. England

C. the Soviet Union

D. Canada

81. What color is a polar bear's skin?

A. Black

B. Brown

C. White

D. Spotted

82. Where was the world's smallest fish discovered?

A. Indonesia

B. Brazil

C. Australia

D. Turkey

83. What is the number one seller at Walmart?

A. Toilet paper

B. Bananas

C. Socks

D. Greeting Cards

84. Halitosis is the medical name for what condition?

A. bad breath

B. baldness

C. smelly feet

D. spots

85. Who founded the League of Nations?

A. Winston Churchill

B. Mackenzie King

C. Woodrow Wilson

D. Jan Smuts

86. Which of the following is not a type of force?

A. acceleration

B. friction

C. gravity

D. magnetic

87. What month did Pearl Harbor occur?

A. May

B. November

C. July

D. December

88. Where did the first hot air Balloon ride take place?

A. Berlin

B. Paris

C. London

D. Madrid

89. In Texas it's illegal to swear in front of what?

A. A child

B. A horse

C. A sheriff

D. A corpse

90. Which is the main substance used to make a crayon?

A. Dye

B. Wax

C. Plastic

D. Chalk

91. What is the biggest artery in the human body?

A. Femoral

B. Aorta

C. Coronary

D. Left Anterior Descending

92. Who sang about being an eggman and a walrus?

A. The Beatles

B. The Eagles

C. The Drivers

D. The Lovers

93. Who wrote songs for The Lion King?

A. Elton John

B. Billy Joel

C. Paul McCartney

D. Stevie Wonder

94. Where is the Sea of Tranquility located?

A. Mars

B. Earth

C. Jupiter

D. The moon

95. What blood type qualifies as a universal donor?

A. B positive

B. A negative

C. AB positive

D. O negative

96. What country has the most vending machines per capita?

A. South Korea

B. Japan

C. China

D. India

97. Botany is the scientific study of what?

A. Flowers

B. Plants

C. Biomes

D. Bugs

98. Which of the following is a nautical unit for speed?

A. cable

B. fathom

C. knot

D. nautical mile

99. In what year was the Civil Rights Act signed?

A. 1968

B. 1965

C. 1964

D. 1963

100. What country has the world's most ancient forest?

A. Germany

B. Canada

C. China

D. Australia

101. What were the two sides in World War II known as?

A. Allies and Axis

B. Allies and Enemies

C. Axis and Nations

D. Axis and Tripartite Alliance

102. In which city was Anne Frank's hiding place?

A. Amsterdam

B. Paris

C. London

D. Brussels

103. Why are hockey pucks frozen before a game?

A. To prevent their breaking up

B. To prevent them from bouncing

C. To add strength

D. To prevent injuries to players

104. Which country is predominantly Buddhist?

A. Thailand

B. Slovakia

C. South Korea

D. Botswana

105. Which building has 73 Elevators?

A. Empire State

B. Bank of America Tower

C. Chrysler Building

D. CN Tower

106. What is the driest continent?

A. Antarctica

B. Africa

C. Arctic

D. Australia

107. According to Greek myth who had snakes for hair?

A. Medusa

B. Venus

C. Artemia

D. Aphrodite

108. Diamonds are made from which element?

A. carbon

B. platinum

C. silicon

D. silver

109. Biscuit is roughly translated to mean what?

A. Fluffy puck

B. Twice cooked

C. Once cooked

D. Soft circle

110. What was Toyota's first popular hybrid car called?

A. Yaris

B. Matrix

C. Prius

D. Camry

111. Which president is responsible for the forward pass?

A. William Howard Taft

B. William McKinley

C. Teddy Roosevelt

D. Franklin D. Roosevelt

112. Who discovered Australia?

A. Christopher Columbus

B. Robert Scott

C. James Cook

D. James Peterson

113. What is the highest active volcano in Europe?

A. Mount Etna

B. Mount Mayon

C. Mount Fiji

D. Mount Stromboli

114. Where was the world's first University located?

A. Alexandria

B. Constantinople

C. Rome

D. Athens

115. What was Marilyn Monroe's natural hair color?

A. Brunette

B. Blonde

C. Black

D. Red

116. What is the national dish of Spain?

A. Queso manchego

B. Tapas

C. Paella

D. Patatas Bravas

117. Which country uses the most renewable energy?

A. Iceland

B. Spain

C. Ireland

D. Finland

118. Which dinosaur had 15 horns?

A. Koreaceratops

B. Kosmoceratops

C. Pachyrhinosaurus

D. Protoceratops

119. How did Anne Frank receive her diary?

A. Birthday gift

B. found it

C. stole it

D. bought it herself

120. The aardvark is native to which continent?

A. Asia

B. South America

C. Oceania

D. Africa

121. Which type of fruit juice did Dole sell first?

A. Cranberry

B. Pineapple

C. Grape

D. Tomato

122. What is the capital of Singapore?

A. Singapore

B. Jurong

C. Serangoon

D. Tampines

123. Where is the Mariana Trench is located?

A. Pacific Ocean

B. Indian Ocean

C. Atlantic Ocean

D. Arctic Ocean

124. Who established the 365-day calendar?

A. Augustus

B. Julius Caesar

C. Trajan

D. Henry VI

125. Which is the lightest chemical element?

A. helium

B. hydrogen

C. lithium

D. nitrogen

126. Which 1998 Disney film was Lindsay Lohan's film debut?

A. Freaky Friday

B. Parent Trap

C. Mean Girls

D. Just My Luck

127. Carrots are a good source of which vitamin?

A. Vitamin C

B. Vitamin B

C. Vitamin E

D. Vitamin A

128. What continent has the most countries?

A. Africa

B. Asia

C. Europe

D. South America

129. What was the first fruit that was eaten on the moon?

A. Apple

B. Plum

C. Melon

D. Peach

130. In which country is the Troi-Rivieres bridge?

A. France

B. Canada

C. Vietnam

D. Algeria

131. Which among these cities is NOT located in Canada?

A. Quebec

B. Montreal

C. Toronto

D. Edinburgh

132. The southern tip of South America has what name?

A. Cape Horn

B. Cape Town

C. Ushuaia

D. Buenos Aires

133. What year did Queen Victoria become Queen?

A. 1845

B. 1829

C. 1835

D. 1837

134. Which dynasty built most of the Great Wall of China?

A. Shang

B. Zhou

C. Ming

D. Yuan

135. In which city did the Napoleonic wars end?

A. Ligny

B. Paris

C. Waterloo

D. Wavre

136. As what type of beans are chickpeas also known as?

A. Great White North

B. Pinto

C. Black

D. Garbanzo

137. How many French Open titles has Rafael Nadal won?

A. 10

B. 8

C. 12

D. 14

138. Which creatures produce gossamer?

A. Silkworms

B. A spider

C. Moths

D. Caterpillars

139. In which U.S. state was the atomic bomb tested in?

A. New York

B. New Mexico

C. Nevada

D. Texas

140. What is the smallest country in the world?

A. Liechtenstein

B. Marshall Islands

C. Vatican City

D. Monaco

141. How many hearts does a worm have?

A. 1

B. 2

C. 3

D. 5

142. Which US city is known as the City of Brotherly Love?

A. Philadelphia

B. Dallas

C. Chicago

D. Boston

143. Danish people live in which country?

A. Denmark

B. Slovenia

C. Dominican Republic

D. Hungary

144. Which mammal has no vocal cords?

A. Giraffe

B. Seals

C. Hippopotamus

D. Walrus

145. The penny-farthing was a popular type of what?

A. Hula-Hoop

B. Flute

C. Bicycle

D. Dance

146. Where was the U.S. largest surrender in battle?

A. Bataan

B. Berlin

C. Paris

D. Tokyo

147. What year was the internet founded?

A. 1980

B. 1990

C. 1989

D. 1988

148. Who started the Russian Revolution?

A. Joseph Stalin

B. Vladimir Lenin

C. Sergei Witte

D. Peter Stolypin

149. A flamboyance is a group of what animals?

A. Doves

B. Dolphins

C. Geese

D. Flamingos

150. What is the capital of India?

A. New Delhi

B. Chennai

C. Jaipur

D. Kolkata

151. What is the fertilized egg of duck is called?

A. Barduk

B. Balut

C. Bantu

D. Barley

152. What is the deepest lake in the world?

A. Lake Michigan

B. Lake Victoria

C. Lake Vostok

D. Lake Baikal

153. Which was the largest tank battle in history?

A. Somme

B. Britain

C. Kursk

D. Stalingrad

154. Which US state has the smallest population?

A. New Mexico

B. Louisiana

C. Maine

D. Wyoming

155. Who is the wife of Zeus?

A. Hera

B. Europa

C. Leda

D. Metis

156. Which of these creatures is an amphibian?

A. agouti

B. horny toad

C. iguana

D. mountain chicken

157. What year was the Seneca Falls Convention?

A. 1845

B. 1830

C. 1848

D. 138

158. What is the main ingredient in falafel?

A. Lentils

B. Rice

C. Chickpea

D. Bulghar

159. Who raised Romulus and Remus?

A. Their parents

B. their grandparents

C. a she-wolf

D. their village

160. An ohm is a measure of what?

A. current

B. power

C. resistance

D. voltage

161. The Ring of Fire is located in which ocean?

A. Indian

B. Atlantic

C. Pacific

D. Arctic

162. How would you write the number 54 in roman numerals?

A. LIV

B. LVI

C. XXXXIV

D. XXXXIIII

163. Which city was Beethoven born in?

A. Bonn

B. Berlin

C. Munich

D. Warsaw

164. What was the first state?

A. Delaware

B. New Jersey

C. Vermont

D. Virginia

165. Who was the first explorer to reach the North Pole?

A. Christopher Columbus

B. James Cook

C. Robert Peary

D. James Clark Ross

166. Which country was the Caesar salad invented in?

A. Italy

B. France

C. United States

D. Mexico

167. Who was childhood friends with Harper Lee?

A. George Orwell

B. Truman Capote

C. Louisa Alcott

D. Jane Austen

168. How many times was Dr. Seuss's first book rejected?

A. 27

B. 30

C. 1

D. 10

169. How many red stripes are there on the American flag?

A. Six

B. Five

C. Seven

D. Eight

170. Where would you find a volcano named Olympus Mons?

A. Greece

B. Pacific Ocean

C. Mars

D. Moon

171. Which are the safest countries for travelers?

A. Iceland

B. Australia

C. India

D. South Korea

172. What currency started in issuing in 2002?

A. Euro

B. Yen

C. Franc

D. Rouble

173. Which country is the largest producer of chocolate?

A. Netherlands

B. United States

C. Australia

D. Germany

174. Which part of the brain interprets light and color?

A. frontal lobe

B. parietal lobe

C. occipital lobe

D. temporal lobe

175. In which city is Jim Morrison buried?

A. London

B. Paris

C. New Orleans

D. Tokyo

176. Which Theatre did Shakespeare create?

A. London Theatre

B. Global Theatre

C. Globe Theatre

D. Essex Theatre

177. What is Japanese sake made from?

A. Soy

B. Barley

C. Rice

D. Wheat

178. Which U.S. state has Garden State as its nickname?

A. New York

B. New Jersey

C. Connecticut

D. Rhode Island

179. Who signed the Magna Carta?

A. King George

B. King William

C. King John

D. Queen Victoria

180. What book starts with the line Call me Ishmael??

A. Brave New World

B. The Plague

C. 100 Years of Solitude

D. Moby Dick

181. Which country has the largest Muslim population?

A. Indonesia

B. Afghanistan

C. Mali

D. Syria

182. What country won the Eurovision Song Contest 2017?

A. Spain

B. Portugal

C. Croatia

D. Sweden

183. What is the main component of Saturn's rings?

A. dust

B. gas

C. ice

D. rock

184. Canberra is the capital city of which country?

A. New Zealand

B. Australia

C. Papau New Guinea

D. Fiji

185. Who was the only US President to resign?

A. Gerald Ford

B. Richard Nixon

C. William McKinley

D. William Taft

186. The Larry O'Brien Championship Trophy is awarded to:

A. The winner of the NBA Finals

B. The Eastern Conference champions

C. The Western Conference champions

D. The Central Division champions

187. What animal is in Bhutan's flag?

A. tiger

B. dragon

C. lion

D. dog

188. What's the most populous city in the United States?

A. New York City

B. Los Angeles

C. Chicago

D. Houston

189. How do you tell the age of a horse?

A. Its teeth

B. Its horseshoe

C. Its hair

D. Its tail

190. Who had the nickname Scarface?

A. Truman Capote

B. Elliot Ness

C. Al Capone

D. Bugsy Siegel

191. What was the name of Alexander the Great's horse?

A. Alexander II

B. Achilles

C. Bucephalus

D. Patrocles

192. Which of the following numbers is a prime number?

A. 6

B. 9

C. 13

D. 15

193. Which art movement is Salvador Dali associated with?

A. Abstract

B. Surrealism

C. Conceptualism

D. Expressionism

194. Who was the first Roman emperor to claim Christianity?

A. Constantine

B. Augustus

C. Licinius

D. Dalmatius

195. How old was Marie Antoinette when she married?

A. 14

B. 13

C. 19

D. 21

196. What sport has been played on the moon?

A. Baseball

B. Bowling

C. Golf

D. Hockey

197. How many provinces does China have?

A. 23

B. 13

C. 10

D. 34

198. Which Saint banished all snakes from Ireland?

A. Patrick

B. Nicholas

C. Paul

D. Anne

199. The Petronas Towers is located in what country?

A. Singapore

B. Indonesia

C. Thailand

D. Malaysia

200. Which animal was the main cause of the Bubonic Plague?

A. Rats

B. Rabbits

C. Cats

D. Birds

Answers

1. Which US state has the longest coastline?

Alaska

2. Which animal was the first animal in space?

Fruit flies

3. What is the longest mountain range in the world?

Andes

4. In which country is divorce illegal?

Philippines

5. Which country is NOT part of the Mediterranean?

Germany

6. What profession did Spartacus have?

Gladiator

7. Where on the human body is the zygomatic bone found?

Facial cheek

8. What is the mass of 1 liter of water?

1 kilogram

9. Which country invented paper?

China

10. What is the lowest army rank of a US soldier?

Private

11. Hepatitis is inflammation of which organ?

Liver

12. Which is the closest star to earth?

Sun

13. Who was the longest-serving U.K. Prime Minister?

Robert Walpole

14. In Roman Myth Mars is the god of what?

War

15. Who developed the theory of relativity?

Albert Einstein

16. What is the largest continent by population?

Asia

17. Who was monarch after Queen Elizabeth I?

James VI

18. Where is the Machu Picchu located?

Peru

19. How many brains does a starfish have?

0

20. What country was formerly referred to as Persia?

Iran

21. In which city does the queen live?

London

22. Who was the first U.S Secretary of Treasury?

Alexander Hamilton

23. Which US state is also called the Aloha State?

Hawaii

24. Which gas makes the bubbles in a soda drink?

Carbon dioxide

25. Who was the cartoonist behind the Far Side Gallery?

Gary Larson

26. How many time zones does the United States have?

9

27. How many faces does a dodecahedron have?

12

28. How many republics were part of the Soviet Union?

15

29. Which is the smallest organ in the human body?

Pineal gland

30. Distance is equal to speed multiplied by what?

Time

31. The Mayans worshiped which animal as gods?

Turkeys

32. Charles Darwin is famous for the theory of what?

Evolution

33. What type of tree grows from an acorn?

Oak

34. Which of these numbers is larger?

Centillion

35. What country did the U.S. buy Alaska
from?

Russia

36. Bicycles were first used in which
country?

Germany

37. What is the Jewish New Year called?

Rosh Hashanah

38. How many years old is the oldest piece of chewing gum?

9,000 years

39. What was banned in Indonesia for stimulating passion?

Hula hoops

40. Which country has the highest agricultural production?

China

41. Who invented the rocking chair?

Benjamin Franklin

42. What is a haboob?

A type of sandstorm

43. Nepal is located on which continent?

Asia

44. In 1979 the USSR invaded which country?

Afghanistan

45. What language has the most words?

English

46. What did Alexander Graham Bell invent?

Telephone

47. How did Fredrick Douglass escape slavery?

Disguised as a sailor

48. Which date was Julius Caesar killed?

March 15th

49. Hemoglobin contains which metal?

Iron

50. Who was the Iron Lady?

Margaret Thatcher

51. What does the Scoville scale measure?

Spiciness of chili peppers

52. What country has competitive office chair racing?

Japan

53. What's the brightest star in the sky?

Sirius

54. Which Philosopher tutored Alexander
the Great?

Aristotle

55. Who did Aaron Burr kill?

Alexander Hamilton

56. In which city did Anne Frank hide from
the Nazis?

Amsterdam

57. Galileo was the citizen of which
country?

Italy

58. Caesar salad originated from which country?

Mexico

59. Which city was the ASPCA founded in?

New York City

60. Madras is now called as which Indian city?

Chennai

61. Where did the Battle of Stalingrad take place?

Soviet Union

62. What year did the Spanish civil war occur?

1936

63. Which country has a flag with only two colors?

Nigeria

64. What is often seen as the smallest unit of memory?

Kilobyte

65. The oldest living person lived in which country?

France

66. The United Kingdom shares a border with which country?

Ireland

67. Julius Caesar was kidnapped by who in 78 BC?

Pirates

68. Which Germany Official ordered the Final Solution?

Goering

69. How many countries have names that end in -stan?

70. An Apgar score is given to what?

Health of newborns

71. The term malar refers to what part of the human body?

Cheek

72. Who introduced the world's first mass-produced car?

Henry Ford

73. Which fruit floats because 25% of its volume is air?

Apple

74. What does an ornithologist study?

Birds

75. What are the two fruit juices in a cosmopolitan?

Cranberry and lime

76. Where did Barack Obama teach constitutional law?

University of Chicago

77. Which University did Karl Marx attend in 1835?

Bonn

78. What is the world's biggest rodent?

Capybara

79. If a male donkey is a jack what is the
female called?

Jenny

80. The space race was between the U.S.
and which country?

The Soviet Union

81. What color is a polar bear's skin?

Black

82. Where was the world's smallest fish discovered?

Indonesia

83. What is the number one seller at Walmart?

Bananas

84. Halitosis is the medical name for what condition?

Bad breath

85. Who founded the League of Nations?

Woodrow Wilson

86. Which of the following is not a type of force?

Acceleration

87. What month did Pearl Harbor occur?

December

88. Where did the first hot air Balloon ride take place?

Paris

89. In Texas it's illegal to swear in front of what?

A corpse

90. Which is the main substance used to make a crayon?

Wax

91. What is the biggest artery in the human body?

Aorta

92. Who sang about being an eggman and a walrus?

The Beatles

93. Who wrote songs for The Lion King?

Elton John

94. Where is the Sea of Tranquility located?

The moon

95. What blood type qualifies as a universal donor?

O negative

96. What country has the most vending machines per capita?

Japan

97. Botany is the scientific study of what?

Plants

98. Which of the following is a nautical unit for speed?

Knot

99. In what year was the Civil Rights Act signed?

1964

100. What country has the world's most ancient forest?

Australia

101. What were the two sides in World War II known as?

Allies and Axis

102. In which city was Anne Frank's hiding place?

Amsterdam

103. Why are hockey pucks frozen before a game?

To prevent them from bouncing

104. Which country is predominantly Buddhist?

Thailand

105. Which building has 73 Elevators?

Empire State

106. What is the driest continent?

Antarctica

107. According to Greek myth who had snakes for hair?

Medusa

108. Diamonds are made from which element?

Carbon

109. Biscuit is roughly translated to mean what?

Twice cooked

110. What was Toyota's first popular hybrid car called?

Prius

111. Which president is responsible for the forward pass?

Teddy Roosevelt

112. Who discovered Australia?

James Cook

113. What is the highest active volcano in
Europe?

Mount Etna

114. Where was the world's first University
located?

Constantinople

115. What was Marilyn Monroe's natural
hair color?

Red

116. What is the national dish of Spain?

Paella

117. Which country uses the most renewable energy?

Iceland

118. Which dinosaur had 15 horns?

Kosmoceratops

119. How did Anne Frank receive her diary?

Birthday gift

120. The aardvark is native to which continent?

Africa

121. Which type of fruit juice did Dole sell first?

Pineapple

122. What is the capital of Singapore?

Singapore

123. Where is the Mariana Trench located?

Pacific Ocean

124. Who established the 365-day calendar?

Julius Caesar

125. Which is the lightest chemical element?

Hydrogen

126. Which 1998 Disney film was Lindsay Lohan's film debut?

Parent Trap

127. Carrots are a good source of which vitamin?

Vitamin A

128. What continent has the most countries?

Africa

129. What was the first fruit that was eaten on the moon?

Peach

130. In which country is the Troi-Rivieres bridge?

Canada

131. Which among these cities is NOT located in Canada?

Edinburgh

132. The southern tip of South America has what name?

Cape Horn

133. What year did Queen Victoria become Queen?

1837

134. Which dynasty built most of the Great Wall of China?

Ming

135. In which city did the Napoleonic wars end?

Waterloo

136. As what type of beans are chickpeas also known as?

Garbanzo

137. How many French Open titles has Rafael Nadal won?

14

138. Which creatures produce gossamer?

A spider

139. In which U.S. state was the atomic bomb tested in?

New Mexico

140. What is the smallest country in the world?

Vatican City

141. How many hearts does a worm have?

5

142. Which US city is known as the City of Brotherly Love?

Philadelphia

143. Danish people live in which country?

Denmark

144. Which mammal has no vocal cords?

Giraffe

145. The penny-farthing was a popular type of what?

Bicycle

146. Where was the U.S. largest surrender in battle?

Bataan

147. What year was the internet founded?

1989

148. Who started the Russian Revolution?

Vladimir Lenin

149. A flamboyance is a group of what animals?

Flamingos

150. What is the capital of India?

New Delhi

151. What is the fertilized egg of duck is called?

Balut

152. What is the deepest lake in the world?

Lake Baikal

153. Which was the largest tank battle in history?

Kursk

154. Which US state has the smallest population?

Wyoming

155. Who is the wife of Zeus?

Hera

156. Which of these creatures is an amphibian?

Mountain chicken

157. What year was the Seneca Falls Convention?

1848

158. What is the main ingredient in falafel?

Chickpea

159. Who raised Romulus and Remus?

A she-wolf

160. An ohm is a measure of what?

Resistance

161. The Ring of Fire is located in which ocean?

Pacific

162. How would you write the number 54 in roman numerals?

LIV

163. Which city was Beethoven born in?

Bonn

164. What was the first state?

Delaware

165. Who was the first explorer to reach the North Pole?

Robert Peary

166. Which country was the Caesar salad invented in?

Mexico

167. Who was childhood friends with Harper Lee?

Truman Capote

168. How many times was Dr. Seuss's first book rejected?

27

169. How many red stripes are there on the American flag?

Seven

170. Where would you find a volcano named Olympus Mons?

Mars

171. Which are the safest countries for travelers?

Iceland

172. What currency started in issuing in 2002?

Euro

173. Which country is the largest producer of chocolate?

Germany

174. Which part of the brain interprets light and color?

Occipital lobe

175. In which city is Jim Morrison buried?

Paris

176. Which Theatre did Shakespeare create?

Globe Theatre

177. What is Japanese sake made from?

Rice

178. Which U.S. state has Garden State as
its nickname?

New Jersey

179. Who signed the Magna Carta?

King John

180. What book starts with the line Call me Ishmael??

Moby Dick

181. Which country has the largest Muslim population?

Indonesia

182. What country won the Eurovision Song Contest 2017?

Portugal

183. What is the main component of Saturn's rings?

Ice

184. Canberra is the capital city of which country?

Australia

185. Who was the only US President to resign?

Richard Nixon

186. The Larry O'Brien Championship Trophy is awarded to:

The winner of the NBA Finals

187. What animal is in Bhutan's flag?

Dragon

188. What's the most populous city in the United States?

New York City

189. How do you tell the age of a horse?

Its teeth

190. Who had the nickname Scarface?

Al Capone

191. What was the name of Alexander the Great's horse?

Bucephalus

192. Which of the following numbers is a prime number?

13

193. Which art movement is Salvador Dali associated with?

Surrealism

194. Who was the first Roman emperor to claim Christianity?

Constantine

195. How old was Marie Antoinette when she married?

14

196. What sport has been played on the moon?

Golf

197. How many provinces does China have?

23

198. Which Saint banished all snakes from Ireland?

Patrick

199. The Petronas Towers is located in what country?

Malaysia

200. Which animal was the main cause of the Bubonic Plague?

Rats

www.ingramcontent.com/pod-product-compliance
Lightning Source LLC
Chambersburg PA
CBHW050821260726
48660CB00004B/1545